50 Ways to Your Hoi Minu

Your Complete Step by Step Guide to Organize Your Home, Clear the Clutter and Live Stress Free

Table of Contents

Introduction

Chapter 1: The Power of Decluttering

Chapter 2: The 10-Minute Rule

Chapter 3: Quick Wins in the Living Room

Chapter 4: Streamlining the Kitchen Chaos

Chapter 5: Bedroom Bliss in Minutes

Chapter 6: Taming the Technology Tornado

Chapter 7: Decluttering for a Sustainable Future

Chapter 8: Maintaining Your Decluttered Home

Conclusion

Introduction

In the hustle and bustle of our daily lives, the spaces we inhabit often mirror the chaos we experience within. The clutter that accumulates in our homes not only creates a physical mess but can also weigh heavily on our mental well-being. If you find yourself yearning for a more organized and stress-free existence, then this guide is your key to unlocking the transformative power of decluttering.

"50 Ways to Declutter Your Home in 50 Minutes" is not just a book; it's a roadmap to reclaiming your space and revitalizing your life. In the following chapters, we will embark on a journey together—one that promises quick and effective strategies to bring order to the chaos that may have taken residence in your home.

Decluttering isn't just about tidying up; it's a profound act of self-care. As you navigate through each chapter, you'll discover the profound impact that a clutter-free environment can have on your mental clarity, productivity, and overall sense of well-being.

We'll introduce you to the concept of the 10-minute rule, a simple yet powerful approach that breaks down decluttering into manageable timeframes. With each passing chapter, you'll explore specific areas of your home, from the living room to the bedroom, and uncover practical tips to streamline and organize.

But our journey doesn't stop there. In the digital age, clutter extends beyond the physical realm. We'll delve into the often-overlooked world of digital clutter and guide you on how to create harmony in your virtual spaces.

Moreover, our exploration goes beyond personal benefits. We'll discuss the symbiotic relationship between decluttering and sustainability, offering eco-friendly solutions to parting ways with items you no longer need.

By the end of this guide, you'll not only have a decluttered home but also the tools to maintain this newfound order. This isn't just about creating an aesthetically pleasing space; it's about fostering an environment that nurtures your well-being and allows you to live stress-free.

Are you ready to embark on this transformative journey? Let's dive into "50 Ways to Declutter Your Home in 50 Minutes" and reclaim the peace and tranquility that should be inherent in the place you call home.

Chapter 1- The Power of Decluttering

1.1 Unveiling the Mental Weight of Clutter

Our journey into the transformative world of decluttering begins by peeling back the layers to reveal the hidden mental weight that clutter imposes on our lives. We explore the psychological intricacies of attachment to possessions, dissecting the reasons we hold onto items long after their utility has waned. As you immerse yourself in the exploration of clutter's mental toll, you'll gain a profound understanding of how our living spaces become reflections of our internal states.

1.2 The Clutter-Stress Connection

In this section, we delve into the research-backed connection between clutter and stress. Studies have shown that a cluttered environment can contribute to elevated stress levels, affecting our mood, focus, and overall well-being. Real-life stories serve as poignant examples, illustrating how the seemingly innocuous accumulation of possessions can exert a significant impact on our mental and emotional states. By understanding this connection, you lay the groundwork for a deliberate and purposeful decluttering journey.

1.3 The Liberation of Letting Go

Decluttering is not merely a physical act; it is a liberating experience—a conscious decision to let go of the unnecessary. Chapter 1 explores the emotional facets of parting ways with possessions. It delves into the freedom that comes with shedding the weight of excess, whether it be material possessions or the emotional baggage associated with them. The philosophy of embracing minimalism is introduced as a pathway to intentional living, inviting you to consider the transformative power of a clutter-free existence.

1.4 The Domino Effect on Well-Being

As you navigate through this chapter, you'll uncover the far-reaching effects of decluttering on your overall well-being. A clutter-free environment becomes a catalyst for mental clarity, unlocking the potential for increased focus and productivity. The soothing impact of a tidy space on stress levels is explored, emphasizing the importance of cultivating a harmonious living environment. By the end of this section, you'll be equipped with the knowledge of how decluttering extends beyond aesthetics, becoming a cornerstone of holistic well-being.

1.5 Setting the Stage for Transformation

In the concluding moments of Chapter 1, the focus shifts to setting the stage for the transformative journey ahead. Decluttering is not a mere chore but a lifestyle shift. This section prepares you for the practical steps and strategies that will follow, encouraging you to embrace the idea that the power of letting go is the key to reclaiming control over your living space. With a heightened awareness of the mental, emotional, and well-being benefits, you turn the page ready to embark on a journey that promises not just a clutter-free home but a rejuvenated and stress-free life.

"50 Ways to Declutter Your Home in 50 Minutes" is not just a book; it's a roadmap to reclaiming your space and revitalizing your life. In the following chapters, we will embark on a journey together—one that promises quick and effective strategies to bring order to the chaos that may have taken residence in your home.

Decluttering isn't just about tidying up; it's a profound act of self-care. As you navigate through each chapter, you'll discover the profound impact that a clutter-free environment can have on your mental clarity, productivity, and overall sense of well-being.

We'll introduce you to the concept of the 10-minute rule, a simple yet powerful approach that breaks down decluttering into manageable timeframes. With each passing chapter, you'll explore specific areas of your home, from the living room to the bedroom, and uncover practical tips to streamline and organize.

But our journey doesn't stop there. In the digital age, clutter extends beyond the physical realm. We'll delve into the often-overlooked world of digital clutter and guide you on how to create harmony in your virtual spaces.

Moreover, our exploration goes beyond personal benefits. We'll discuss the symbiotic relationship between decluttering and sustainability, offering eco-friendly solutions to parting ways with items you no longer need.

By the end of this guide, you'll not only have a decluttered home but also the tools to maintain this newfound order. This isn't just about creating an aesthetically pleasing space; it's about fostering an environment that nurtures your well-being and allows you to live stress-free.

Are you ready to embark on this transformative journey? Let's dive into "50 Ways to Declutter Your Home in 50 Minutes" and reclaim the peace and tranquility that should be inherent in the place you call home.

Chapter 2- The 10-Minute Rule

In the vast landscape of decluttering, one powerful and transformative concept emerges—The 10-Minute Rule. This chapter is an exploration of the magic that lies within the simplicity of breaking down decluttering tasks into manageable increments. Prepare to embark on a journey where each 10-minute segment becomes a stepping stone to a clutter-free haven.

2.1 The Genesis of the 10-Minute Rule

To understand the potency of the 10-Minute Rule, we delve into its origins and the psychological underpinnings that make it an effective strategy. Unpacking the science behind small, consistent efforts, we explore how this rule bypasses the overwhelm often associated with decluttering. You'll discover how breaking down tasks into bite-sized pieces not only makes them more approachable but also sets the stage for sustainable progress.

2.2 Overcoming Procrastination with Micro-Actions

Procrastination, the nemesis of progress, often lurks in the shadows of decluttering endeavors. Chapter 2 shines a light on how the 10-Minute Rule becomes a powerful weapon against procrastination. By embracing micro-actions, you'll learn how to outsmart the tendency to delay, making consistent and tangible strides towards your decluttering goals.

2.3 The Art of Task Segmentation

This section is a deep dive into the art of segmenting tasks. We explore how seemingly Herculean decluttering projects can be dismantled into manageable components. From tackling a cluttered closet to organizing a chaotic workspace, the 10-Minute Rule becomes your guide, showing you how to navigate the labyrinth of tasks one small step at a time.

2.4 Emotional Resonance of Incremental Progress

The emotional resonance of incremental progress cannot be understated. Chapter 2 uncovers the satisfaction and motivation that accompany each completed 10-minute decluttering session. As you witness tangible changes in your living space, a sense of accomplishment becomes a driving force, propelling you forward on this transformative journey.

2.5 Integrating the Rule into Daily Life

Practicality meets philosophy in this section, as we explore ways to seamlessly integrate the 10-Minute Rule into your daily routine. Whether you're a busy professional, a parent juggling multiple responsibilities, or someone seeking balance in a hectic schedule, you'll discover how this rule becomes a flexible and adaptable tool for reclaiming control over your living space, one incremental step at a time.

2.6 Real-Life Success Stories

To further illustrate the transformative impact of the 10-Minute Rule, this chapter features real-life success stories from individuals who have embraced this approach. Through their experiences, you'll glean inspiration and insights, understanding that the magic of incremental progress is not confined to theory but is a tangible and achievable reality.

2.7 Overcoming Challenges and Resistance

No journey is without its challenges, and decluttering is no exception. Chapter 2 addresses common obstacles and resistance that may arise when implementing the 10-Minute Rule. By offering practical strategies to overcome these hurdles, you'll be equipped with the tools to navigate the twists and turns of your decluttering adventure.

2.8 The Transformative Power of Consistency

As the chapter draws to a close, we reflect on the transformative power of consistency. Each 10-minute decluttering session, seemingly insignificant on its own, contributes to a cumulative effect that reshapes your living space and, by extension, your life. You'll leave Chapter 2 not only with a deep understanding of the 10-Minute Rule but also with a newfound appreciation for the incremental progress that fuels the decluttering journey.

As you turn the page to Chapter 3, armed with the wisdom of the 10-Minute Rule, you'll be ready to embark on practical decluttering adventures that promise to bring about lasting change in your home and life.

Here are 20 bonus tips to complement Chapter 2 and enhance your decluttering journey through the 10-Minute Rule:

Create a Decluttering Playlist:

Compile a motivating playlist that you can play during your 10-minute decluttering sessions. Music can add a positive vibe and make the process more enjoyable.

Use a Timer:

Set a timer for 10 minutes to create a sense of urgency and focus. Knowing you have a limited time can make the task feel more manageable.

Visualize the End Result:

Before starting each session, visualize how you want the space to look after decluttering. This mental image can serve as motivation.

Invite a Decluttering Buddy:

Share the decluttering journey with a friend or family member. Having a buddy can make the process more enjoyable and provide mutual support.

Celebrate Small Wins:

Acknowledge and celebrate each small accomplishment. Treat yourself to a small reward after completing a certain number of sessions.

Designate a Donation Box:

Keep a designated box for items you plan to donate. This makes it easy to declutter while also contributing to a good cause.

Focus on One Area at a Time:

Instead of feeling overwhelmed by the entire space, concentrate on one specific area during each 10-minute session.

Implement the Reverse Hanger Technique:

In your closet, turn all hangers backward. After wearing an item, hang it back the correct way. After a few months, you'll easily identify clothes you don't wear.

Digital Decluttering:

Apply the 10-Minute Rule to digital spaces. Tackle your email inbox, organize files on your computer, and delete unnecessary apps on your phone.

Create a Decluttering Calendar:

Plan your decluttering sessions on a calendar. This adds structure and helps you stay consistent.

Declutter During TV Commercials:

Use commercial breaks as opportunities for quick decluttering. It's a productive way to utilize those short intervals.

Practice the "One In, One Out" Rule:

For every new item you bring into your home, consider removing one. This maintains balance and prevents future clutter.

Embrace the KonMari Method:

Apply Marie Kondo's principles by asking yourself if each item sparks joy. If not, consider letting it go.

Rotate Seasonal Items:

Store seasonal items out of sight when not in use. Rotate them during specific times of the year to keep your space fresh and clutter-free.

Utilize Vertical Space:

Maximize storage by using vertical space, such as wall-mounted shelves or hooks. This not only declutters but also adds a decorative touch.

Digitize Paper Clutter:

Scan and digitize important documents to reduce paper clutter. Create digital folders for easy access.

Declutter Multipurpose Spaces First:

If you have areas that serve multiple purposes (e.g., home office and guest room), declutter these spaces first for maximum impact.

Practice Mindful Decluttering:

Be intentional during each 10-minute session. Ask yourself if an item adds value to your life and contributes to the vision you have for your space.

Set Decluttering Themes:

Assign themes to your decluttering sessions. For example, dedicate one session to books, another to clothing, and so on.

Document Your Journey:

Keep a decluttering journal or take photos before and after each session. Documenting your progress can be motivating and provide a sense of accomplishment.

As you integrate these bonus tips into your decluttering toolkit, the 10-Minute Rule becomes not only a strategy but a lifestyle—a pathway to a clutter-free and harmonious living space.

Chapter 3- Quick Wins in the Living Room

In Chapter 3, we embark on a focused decluttering journey within the heart of your home—the living room. This space, often a hub of activity and relaxation, becomes our canvas for implementing transformative strategies that promise not only quick wins but a lasting sense of order and calm.

3.1 The Living Room as a Reflection of Lifestyle

Begin by understanding the unique role your living room plays in your lifestyle. Explore how this space serves as a gathering point for family, relaxation, and entertainment. Recognizing the diverse functions of the living room sets the stage for targeted and effective decluttering.

3.2 The Art of Furniture Arrangement

Delve into the nuances of furniture arrangement. Learn how the placement of sofas, chairs, and tables can impact the flow of the room. Explore strategies to optimize seating, create focal points, and ensure that the arrangement aligns with both aesthetics and functionality.

3.3 Tackling Entertainment Centers and Cables

Unravel the complexities of entertainment centers and the web of cables that often accompany them. Explore practical tips for decluttering media consoles, organizing DVDs, and managing cables to create a streamlined and visually pleasing entertainment area.

3.4 Decluttering Decor: Striking the Right Balance

Navigate the world of decor and strike a balance between a curated and clutter-free living room. Explore the principles of minimalist design, emphasizing the idea that less can indeed be more. Learn how to showcase meaningful decor while avoiding overcrowding.

3.5 Organizing Bookshelves and Display Units

Dive into the world of bookshelves and display units. Discover strategies for categorizing books, arranging decorative items, and maintaining a cohesive look. This section not only focuses on decluttering but also on creating visually appealing and organized shelving.

3.6 Maximizing Storage Solutions

Explore innovative storage solutions that maximize space while keeping clutter at bay. From stylish storage ottomans to multifunctional furniture pieces, learn how to integrate practical storage without compromising on the aesthetic appeal of your living room.

3.7 The Power of Decluttering Sentimental Items

Navigate the emotional realm of sentimental items within your living room. Discover how to curate and display sentimental pieces without overwhelming the space. This section encourages intentional choices, allowing you to cherish meaningful items while maintaining a clutter-free environment.

3.8 Lighting: Illuminating a Clutter-Free Space

Illuminate your living room, both figuratively and literally, by exploring the impact of lighting on clutter perception. Learn how strategic lighting choices can enhance the ambiance of your space while drawing attention away from potential clutter.

3.9 Integrating Indoor Plants for a Breath of Fresh Air

Dive into the world of indoor plants and their transformative effects on living spaces. Explore how incorporating greenery not only adds aesthetic appeal but also contributes to a healthier environment. Discover low-maintenance plant options ideal for a clutter-free living room.

3.10 Maintaining a Clutter-Free Living Room Routine

Conclude the chapter by establishing routines and habits to maintain the decluttered haven you've created. From daily quick tidying sessions to periodic deep cleans, learn how consistency is key to preserving the order and tranquility of your living room.

As you immerse yourself in the detailed strategies of Chapter 3, envision the transformation of your living room into a harmonious and clutter-free haven—a space that reflects your lifestyle and invites relaxation and connection. With each section offering practical insights, you'll be equipped to implement transformative changes that go beyond quick wins, laying the foundation for a lasting decluttered living space.

Here are 20 bonus tips to complement the strategies outlined in Chapter 3 and further enhance the decluttering process in your living room:

Create a "Clutter Basket":

Place a basket in the living room where items that don't belong can be quickly gathered during a brief tidy-up. Return items to their proper places at the end of the day.

Invest in Multi-Functional Furniture:

Choose furniture that serves multiple purposes, such as a coffee table with storage or ottomans that can double as seating.

Implement a No-Duplicate Rule:

Avoid having duplicates of items in the living room. One set of coasters, one blanket, one set of decorative items—this reduces visual clutter.

Rotate Decor Seasonally:

Keep decor fresh by rotating seasonal items. This not only prevents monotony but also allows for a more intentional display of items.

Utilize Hidden Storage:

Explore furniture with hidden storage compartments, such as sofas with built-in storage or coffee tables with drawers. This keeps essentials close by but out of sight.

Establish a "Daily Reset" Routine:

Dedicate a few minutes each evening to reset the living room. Tidy up cushions, fold blankets, and return any items to their designated spots.

Organize Remote Controls:

Use a stylish remote control organizer or caddy to keep all remotes in one easily accessible place, preventing them from cluttering the coffee table.

Implement a "One-In, One-Out" Rule for Decor:

When introducing new decor items, follow the rule of removing one existing item. This maintains a balanced and intentional decor scheme.

Create a Charging Station:

Designate an area for charging electronic devices. This prevents a tangle of charging cables and ensures devices are ready for use when needed.

Curate a Display Shelf:

Dedicate a shelf for rotating displays of meaningful items. This could include family photos, travel souvenirs, or small art pieces.

Consider Floating Shelves:

Install floating shelves on walls to display decor without taking up floor space. These can be used for books, plants, or decorative items.

Optimize Coffee Table Space:

Keep the coffee table clutter-free by limiting the number of items on display. Prioritize items like a centerpiece or a couple of books for a clean look.

Hang Curtains Strategically:

Hang curtains high and wide to create the illusion of larger windows and a more spacious living room. This enhances the overall sense of openness.

Organize Media Storage:

Streamline your media storage by categorizing DVDs, CDs, or gaming consoles. Use storage bins or cabinets to keep everything in order.

Dedicate a Toy Storage Area:

If the living room is a family space, designate a specific area for toy storage. Use baskets or bins that are easily accessible for quick cleanup.

Implement a "Paperless" System:

Minimize paper clutter by digitizing important documents. Utilize apps or cloud storage for bills, documents, and other paperwork.

Create a Reading Nook:

Designate a cozy corner for reading with a comfortable chair and a small bookshelf. This focused space can help prevent books from scattering throughout the room.

Artful Cord Management:

Use cable organizers or decorative cord covers to manage and conceal electronic cables. This adds a touch of organization to your entertainment area.

Rotate Cushion Covers:

Extend the life of your cushions and change the look of your living room by rotating and washing cushion covers regularly.

Maintain Greenery:

Integrate low-maintenance indoor plants into your living room. Plants not only add freshness but also contribute to a calming atmosphere.

Incorporating these bonus tips alongside the strategies in Chapter 3 will elevate your living room decluttering experience, creating a space that is not only organized but also tailored to your lifestyle and aesthetic preferences.

Chapter 4- Streamlining the Kitchen Chaos

In Chapter 4, we embark on a meticulous journey through the heart of every home—the kitchen. This culinary sanctuary is often a bustling hub, and in its chaos lies the potential for organization and efficiency. Detailed strategies unfold as we explore ways to streamline every nook and cranny, creating a kitchen that not only looks impeccable but functions seamlessly.

4.1 The Functionality Matrix: Understanding Your Kitchen's Needs

Begin with a comprehensive analysis of your kitchen's functionality. Identify zones for food preparation, cooking, storage, and cleaning. Tailor your decluttering efforts to the unique needs of each zone, ensuring that the kitchen becomes a harmonious and purposeful space.

4.2 Decluttering Countertops: A Blank Canvas for Culinary Creativity

Dive into the art of decluttering countertops—the epicenter of kitchen activity. Discover the transformative impact of a clear and open workspace. From minimizing small appliances to organizing utensils, this section unveils practical strategies to create a clutter-free and inspiring kitchen environment.

4.3 Organizing Cabinets and Drawers: A Symphony of Order

Explore the inner sanctums of your kitchen—cabinets and drawers. Uncover strategies for categorizing cookware, utensils, and pantry items. Implement organizational tools, such as drawer dividers and cabinet organizers, to maintain order and make every item easily accessible.

4.4 Taming the Tupperware Tornado: Mastering Container Chaos

Enter the realm of Tupperware and conquer the notorious chaos it often brings. Learn efficient ways to organize containers and lids, bid farewell to mismatched pairs, and implement storage solutions that bring an end to the Tupperware pandemonium.

4.5 The Art of Pantry Optimization: A Feast for the Eyes and Palate

Venture into the pantry and transform it into a well-organized haven. Explore innovative storage solutions, create a system for labeling, and master the art of restocking to ensure your pantry becomes a visual delight and a practical resource for culinary endeavors.

4.6 Refrigerator Revitalization: A Fresh Start for Fresh Ingredients

Open the doors to your refrigerator and embark on a journey of revitalization. From arranging shelves logically to organizing produce, delve into the intricacies of fridge organization. Implement strategies to minimize food waste and create a space where every ingredient has its designated place.

4.7 Mastering Meal Prep: Efficiency in Every Slice

Unlock the secrets of efficient meal prep by organizing your kitchen for streamlined cooking sessions. Discover how to optimize tools, arrange ingredients for easy access, and create a systematic approach to meal preparation that saves time and reduces stress.

4.8 The Dishwashing Dilemma: A Chore Turned Ritual

Transform dishwashing from a chore into a ritual by organizing the kitchen sink area. Explore strategies for efficient dish storage, managing cleaning supplies, and creating a pleasant ambiance that turns the dishwashing routine into a mindful and enjoyable activity.

4.9 Efficient Storage for Small Kitchens: A Symphony in Limited Space

For those navigating the challenges of a small kitchen, this section provides tailored strategies. Explore space-saving solutions, utilize vertical storage, and master the art of decluttering to make the most of every inch in compact culinary spaces.

4.10 Sustainable Kitchen Practices: Nourishing the Planet and Your Space

Conclude the chapter by exploring sustainable practices in the kitchen. Learn how to reduce waste, implement recycling systems, and choose eco-friendly kitchen products. Embrace a kitchen that not only nourishes your family but also contributes to a healthier planet.

As you immerse yourself in the detailed strategies of Chapter 4, envision the transformation of your kitchen into a culinary haven—one that not only delights the senses but also functions as a model of efficiency and order. With each section offering practical insights, you'll be equipped to implement transformative changes that elevate your kitchen to new heights of organization and functionality.

Here are 20 bonus creative tips to complement the strategies outlined in Chapter 4 and infuse your kitchen decluttering journey with innovation and flair:

Repurpose Vintage Items:

Give old kitchen items a new life. Turn vintage crates into stylish spice racks or use vintage mason jars for countertop storage.

Create a Magnetic Spice Wall:

Transform an empty wall into a magnetic spice rack. Attach magnetic containers for easy access and a visually striking display.

DIY Drawer Organizers:

Craft custom drawer organizers using materials like cardboard, foam board, or even repurposed wooden wine boxes. Tailor them to fit your utensils and kitchen tools perfectly.

Chalkboard Labels:

Use chalkboard labels on containers and jars for a dynamic and changeable labeling system. It adds a touch of creativity while allowing for easy updates.

Floating Shelves with a Twist:

Install floating shelves with built-in hooks underneath. Hang mugs or utensils for a functional and visually appealing storage solution.

Patterned Shelf Liners:

Elevate your shelf game with patterned or colorful shelf liners. Not only do they protect your shelves, but they also add a pop of creativity to your cabinets.

Color-Coordinated Storage Bins:

Introduce color-coded storage bins in your pantry or cabinets. Assign each color to a specific category, making it easy to locate items at a glance.

Vintage Tray Turned Organizer:

Repurpose a vintage tray as a stylish organizer on the countertop. Use it to corral frequently used items like salt and pepper shakers or cooking oils.

Herb Garden Window:

Create a mini herb garden on your kitchen windowsill. Use decorative pots and labels for an aesthetic and functional addition to your cooking space.

Hidden Charging Station:

Transform a kitchen drawer into a hidden charging station. Install outlets inside the drawer to keep devices charged without cluttering the countertop.

Utensil Wall Art:

Arrange kitchen utensils on the wall in an artistic pattern. Turn functional items into a visual statement while keeping them within easy reach.

Mismatched Jars as Drinkware:

Embrace a quirky aesthetic by using mismatched jars as drinking glasses. It adds a touch of eclecticism to your kitchen and reduces the need for dedicated glassware.

DIY Hanging Pot Rack:

Craft a hanging pot rack using a wooden ladder or repurposed pipes. This creative solution not only saves cabinet space but also adds an industrial-chic vibe.

Mini Chalkboard Menu:

Hang a mini chalkboard in the kitchen to showcase the weekly menu. It adds a personalized touch and helps with meal planning.

Vintage Cookbook Display:

Display vintage cookbooks as decorative elements. Prop them up on shelves or use book stands for a nostalgic and functional kitchen accent.

Pegboard Wall Organizer:

Install a pegboard on an empty kitchen wall. Use pegs and hooks to organize utensils, cutting boards, and even small pots and pans.

DIY Hanging Fruit Basket:

Create a hanging fruit basket using wire baskets or repurposed containers. Hang it from the ceiling for a unique and space-saving fruit storage solution.

Glass Jar Pendant Lights:

Turn glass jars into pendant lights above the kitchen island. It's a creative way to add unique lighting while repurposing everyday items.

Customizable Recipe Board:

Create a customizable recipe board on the kitchen wall. Use magnetic boards or corkboards to display favorite recipes, grocery lists, and meal plans.

Magnetic Knife Strip as a Utensil Organizer:

Utilize a magnetic knife strip to organize metal utensils. It adds an industrial-chic element to the kitchen while keeping your tools within easy reach.

Incorporate these creative tips into your kitchen decluttering journey to infuse personality and innovation into every corner of your culinary haven.

Chapter 5- Bedroom Bliss in Minutes

In Chapter 5, our focus turns to the bedroom—the sanctuary where rest and rejuvenation take center stage. We delve into strategies that transcend mere tidiness, guiding you in the art of creating a tranquil oasis where every element contributes to a restful and harmonious atmosphere.

5.1 The Essence of a Tranquil Bedroom

Begin by exploring the essence of a tranquil bedroom. Understand the symbiotic relationship between an organized space and restful sleep. This section delves into the principles of minimalism, soft color palettes, and the importance of personal touches that make your bedroom a haven of tranquility.

5.2 Decluttering the Sleep Environment: A Canvas of Calm

Embark on a journey to declutter the sleep environment. Discover strategies for organizing bedside tables, minimizing electronic distractions, and creating a soothing ambiance that invites relaxation. Learn the art of curating a serene backdrop that sets the stage for restorative sleep.

5.3 Wardrobe Wellness: A Mindful Approach to Clothing

Navigate the wardrobe with a mindful approach to clothing. Explore techniques for decluttering closets, organizing clothes by category, and implementing storage solutions that maximize space. Transform your wardrobe into a curated collection that promotes ease and simplicity in your daily routine.

5.4 Linen Luxury: Elevating Bedding to a New Standard

Delve into the world of linen luxury as we explore ways to elevate your bedding to a new standard. From choosing calming color schemes to incorporating textures and layers, learn how to create a sumptuous bed that beckons you into a restful embrace every night.

5.5 Personalized Retreats: Adding Your Signature Touch

Infuse your bedroom with personal touches that transform it into a truly personalized retreat. Explore ideas for creating a gallery wall with meaningful artwork, arranging sentimental items, and incorporating elements that resonate with your unique style. Your bedroom becomes a canvas for self-expression and serenity.

5.6 Technology Detox: Nurturing the Sleep Environment

Implement a technology detox in the bedroom. Learn how to create zones free from screens, establish calming bedtime rituals, and invest in sleep-promoting accessories. This section guides you in fostering an environment that encourages quality sleep and rejuvenation.

5.7 Zenful Zeniths: Mindful Furniture Arrangement

Master the art of mindful furniture arrangement to optimize the flow of energy in your bedroom. Explore Feng Shui principles and discover how the strategic placement of furniture contributes to a harmonious and tranquil atmosphere. Your bedroom transforms into a space where positive energy abounds.

5.8 Creating a Reading Nook: Literary Escapes within Reach

Craft a reading nook within your bedroom, turning it into a literary escape. Explore cozy seating options, innovative book storage solutions, and lighting techniques that enhance the reading experience. Your bedroom becomes a haven not just for sleep but for quiet moments of literary bliss.

5.9 Aromatherapy Ambiance: Scents for Serenity

Uncover the world of aromatherapy and its transformative effects on your sleep environment. Explore calming scents, essential oil diffusers, and rituals that enhance relaxation. Your bedroom transcends the visual and becomes a sensory oasis for a restful night's sleep.

5.10 Sustainable Sleep: Eco-Friendly Practices

Conclude the chapter by embracing sustainable sleep practices. Explore eco-friendly bedding options, energy-efficient lighting, and ways to minimize environmental impact in your bedroom. Your tranquil oasis becomes not only a haven for rest but also a space that aligns with eco-conscious living.

As you immerse yourself in the detailed strategies of Chapter 5, envision your bedroom transforming into a serene sanctuary—a place where order, tranquility, and personalized touches converge to create an environment conducive to restful and rejuvenating sleep.

Here are 20 bonus tips to complement the strategies outlined in Chapter 5 and enhance the organization of your bedroom:

Under-Bed Storage Solutions:

Utilize the space under your bed for storage by using bins, drawers, or a bed with built-in storage. This is perfect for seasonal clothing, extra bedding, or items not frequently used.

Jewelry Wall Display:

Create an organized and visually appealing display for your jewelry on the wall. Install hooks, racks, or a corkboard to keep necklaces, earrings, and accessories easily accessible.

Drawer Dividers for Lingerie:

Use drawer dividers to keep lingerie, socks, and accessories neatly separated. This not only makes it easy to find items but also maintains order within your dresser.

Mindful Nightstand:

Keep your nightstand clutter-free by including only essentials such as a lamp, a book, or a journal. Use drawers for additional storage and to maintain a serene bedside environment.

Seasonal Closet Rotation:

Rotate your wardrobe seasonally. Store out-of-season clothing in bins or vacuum-sealed bags to free up space and keep your closet organized.

Task Lighting for Reading Nook:

Install task lighting in your reading nook to create a cozy atmosphere. Adjustable wall sconces or a reading lamp provide focused illumination for late-night reading.

Daily Clothing Prep Station:

Create a designated area for planning your daily outfits. Use a clothing rack or hooks to organize the next day's attire, streamlining your morning routine.

Cord Organizers:

Tame electronic cords using organizers or clips. This prevents a tangled mess and maintains a clean and organized look around bedside tables or desks.

Memory Box:

Dedicate a memory box for sentimental items like cards, letters, or small mementos. It provides a designated space to cherish memories without cluttering your bedroom.

Minimalist Wall Decor:

Embrace minimalist wall decor to maintain a serene ambiance. Select a few meaningful pieces that contribute to the overall tranquility of the bedroom.

Shoe Storage Solutions:

Keep shoes organized with designated storage solutions. Shoe racks, shelves, or an over-the-door organizer can prevent footwear from cluttering the bedroom floor.

Bookshelf Headboard:

Opt for a bed with a built-in bookshelf as a headboard. It serves as both functional storage and a stylish element for your bedroom.

Vertical Space Utilization:

Maximize vertical space with tall dressers or floor-to-ceiling shelves. This helps in organizing items without taking up excessive floor space.

Essential Oils Diffuser:

Enhance the atmosphere with an essential oil diffuser. Use calming scents like lavender or chamomile to promote relaxation and better sleep.

Mirror Placement for Light Enhancement:

Strategically place mirrors to reflect natural light and make the bedroom appear brighter. This contributes to a spacious and airy feel.

Bedside Basket for Reading Material:

Keep your current reading materials organized in a bedside basket or hanging organizer. It ensures your reading nook stays clutter-free and easily accessible.

Color-Coded Hangers:

Use color-coded hangers to categorize your clothing. This simple visual cue can make your closet look more organized and help you locate specific items effortlessly.

Customized Drawer Labels:

Label your dresser drawers with customized tags or labels. This adds a personal touch and ensures each drawer has a designated purpose.

Fold and Store Off-Season Blankets:

Fold and store off-season blankets in decorative bins or vacuum-sealed bags. This keeps your bedroom free from unnecessary bulk and maintains a cozy feel.

Adjustable Shelving for Flexibility:

Opt for adjustable shelving in your closet or storage units. This allows you to adapt the space based on your evolving organizational needs and the changing seasons.

Incorporating these bonus tips into your bedroom organization plan will not only enhance the aesthetic appeal but also contribute to the overall tranquility and functionality of your personal haven.

Chapter 6- Taming the Technology Tornado

In Chapter 6, we address the omnipresent challenge of managing the technology tornado that swirls around our lives. Dive into comprehensive strategies aimed at regaining control, decluttering digital spaces, and establishing a harmonious relationship with technology that promotes efficiency and peace of mind.

6.1 Understanding the Digital Onslaught

Begin by comprehending the scope of the digital onslaught. Explore the various aspects of technology contributing to the feeling of overwhelm, including emails, files, apps, and electronic devices. Acknowledge the challenges before diving into effective solutions.

6.2 Inbox Zen: Taming Email Overload

Embark on a journey to achieve inbox zen by taming email overload. Implement strategies for organizing emails, setting up filters and labels, and creating a systematic approach to managing your digital communication. Transform your inbox into a streamlined and efficient communication hub.

6.3 File Feng Shui: Organizing Digital Documents

Apply the principles of file Feng Shui to bring order to your digital documents. Explore techniques for categorizing files, creating a logical folder structure, and implementing naming conventions that facilitate easy retrieval. Transform your digital filing system into a well-organized and efficient repository.

6.4 App Detox: Streamlining Your Digital Toolkit

Navigate the world of apps and perform a thorough app detox. Learn to assess which apps serve a purpose and contribute to your productivity. Organize apps into folders, remove redundant ones, and create a digital toolkit that aligns with your workflow and goals.

6.5 Cloud Clarity: Maximizing Digital Storage

Gain cloud clarity by optimizing your digital storage solutions. Explore cloud platforms, backup strategies, and synchronization options to ensure seamless access to your files across devices. This section guides you in harnessing the power of the cloud while maintaining security and order.

6.6 Device Harmony: Managing Multiple Gadgets

Achieve device harmony by effectively managing multiple gadgets. Explore synchronization options, declutter home screens, and implement a unified system for managing devices. Learn to maintain consistency across smartphones, tablets, and other electronic tools.

6.7 Password Mastery: Enhancing Security and Efficiency

Master the art of password management to enhance both security and efficiency. Explore password manager tools, create strong and unique passwords, and streamline the login process across different accounts. This section ensures that your digital accounts are secure and easily accessible.

6.8 Digital Downtime: Establishing Boundaries

Explore the concept of digital downtime to establish healthy boundaries. Learn strategies for minimizing screen time, setting device-free zones, and cultivating mindful habits that contribute to a balanced and fulfilling life. This section encourages a conscious and intentional approach to technology usage.

6.9 Notifications Navigated: Minimizing Distractions

Navigate the world of notifications to minimize distractions. Explore customization options for app notifications, establish notification schedules, and create an environment that allows you to focus without constant interruptions. This section guides you in reclaiming control over your attention.

6.10 Future-Proofing: Adapting to Technological Changes

Conclude the chapter by exploring strategies for future-proofing your digital organization. Stay informed about technological advancements, continuously assess and refine your digital systems, and embrace a mindset that adapts to changes in the digital landscape. This section ensures that your digital organization remains efficient and relevant over time.

As you immerse yourself in the detailed strategies of Chapter 6, envision a transformed digital landscape—one where technology becomes a tool for empowerment rather than a source of chaos. Taming the technology tornado is not only about decluttering digital spaces but also about fostering a healthy and intentional relationship with the digital world.

Here are 20 creative bonus tips to complement the strategies outlined in Chapter 6 and help you tame the technology tornado with flair:

Digital Vision Board:

Create a digital vision board on your computer or tablet. Use inspiring images, quotes, and goals as your wallpaper to stay motivated and focused.

Customized Desktop Icons:

Personalize your desktop icons with custom images or designs. This adds a touch of creativity to your digital workspace and makes it more visually appealing.

Interactive Screensaver:

Set an interactive screensaver that displays your to-do list, calendar, or motivational quotes. Make your screensaver a dynamic and useful part of your workspace.

Color-Coded Folders:

Assign specific colors to folders based on categories or priority levels. This visual organization makes it easier to identify and access files quickly.

Digital Mind Map:

Create a digital mind map using apps or software to visually organize your thoughts, ideas, and projects. It's a creative way to brainstorm and plan.

Tech-Free Break Corner:

Designate a tech-free corner in your home office for breaks. Include a cozy chair, a plant, or a vision board to create a relaxing and inspiring space.

Themed Digital Calendars:

Customize your digital calendar with themes for each month. It could be colors, patterns, or images that change regularly, adding a creative touch to your schedule.

Animated Reminders:

Use animated GIFs or short videos as reminders for important tasks. This playful approach can make your reminders more engaging and memorable.

Digital Sticky Notes Art:

Turn your digital sticky notes into art by arranging them creatively on your desktop. This can serve as a functional and artistic way to organize your thoughts.

Innovative Keyboard Shortcuts:

Create custom keyboard shortcuts for frequently used applications or commands. This not only saves time but also adds a tech-savvy element to your workflow.

DIY Charging Station:

Design and build your own DIY charging station for your devices. Customize it with materials that match your home office decor for a stylish tech solution.

Interactive Whiteboard Software:

Use interactive whiteboard software to jot down ideas, sketch, or make notes during virtual meetings. It's a dynamic way to enhance collaboration and creativity.

Digital Detox Playlist:

Create a playlist specifically for your digital detox sessions. Music can help set the tone for a break from screens and promote relaxation.

AR Workspace Enhancements:

Explore augmented reality (AR) apps that enhance your workspace. Virtual post-it notes, 3D models, or interactive elements can make your digital space more dynamic.

Voice Command Customization:

Personalize voice commands for your virtual assistant or voice-activated devices. Make it fun and unique to add a touch of personality to your tech interactions.

Interactive Screens:

If possible, invest in touch-screen monitors or tablets for your home office. It adds a hands-on, interactive element to your digital workspace.

Digital Art Gallery:

Turn your computer or tablet into a digital art gallery by displaying rotating artwork as your screensaver. It's a visually stimulating way to take breaks.

Virtual Commute Routine:

Establish a virtual commute routine by using a relaxation app or a short mindfulness video before and after your work hours. It helps create mental boundaries.

Customized Keyboard Covers:

Personalize your keyboard by using customized keyboard covers. Choose colors, patterns, or even motivational quotes to make your workspace uniquely yours.

Digital Scent Diffuser:

Explore digital scent diffusers that sync with your workspace ambiance. Choose scents that boost focus or relaxation to enhance your overall digital experience.

Incorporating these creative bonus tips into your technology management strategies will not only add a personal touch but also infuse a sense of fun and innovation into your digital workspace.

Chapter 7- Decluttering for a Sustainable Future

In Chapter 7, our focus shifts towards decluttering with a purpose beyond personal organization – it's about embracing sustainable practices that not only benefit your immediate surroundings but contribute to a healthier planet. Explore strategies to minimize waste, make eco-friendly choices, and cultivate a mindful approach to decluttering for a sustainable and harmonious future.

7.1 The Environmental Impact of Clutter

Begin by understanding the environmental impact of clutter. Explore how excess possessions contribute to resource depletion, increased waste, and environmental strain. Acknowledge the role of mindful decluttering in fostering a sustainable lifestyle.

7.2 Mindful Sorting: Reduce, Reuse, Recycle

Embark on a journey of mindful sorting as you declutter. Implement the principles of reduce, reuse, and recycle. Prioritize items that can be repurposed or recycled, and explore opportunities to minimize waste in the decluttering process.

7.3 Upcycling Unwanted Items: From Clutter to Creativity

Discover the art of upcycling as a transformative decluttering strategy. Explore creative ways to repurpose items that might otherwise be discarded. From turning old furniture into new pieces to transforming clothing into DIY projects, infuse your decluttering journey with a touch of creativity and sustainability.

7.4 Sustainable Storage Solutions: Eco-Friendly Organization

Delve into sustainable storage solutions that align with your commitment to eco-friendly living. Explore materials such as bamboo, recycled plastic, or reclaimed wood for storage containers and furniture. Implement organization systems that not only declutter but also contribute to a sustainable future.

7.5 The Capsule Concept: Sustainable Wardrobes

Apply the capsule wardrobe concept to declutter and embrace sustainable fashion. Curate a collection of versatile, timeless pieces that can be mixed and matched. By adopting a minimalist approach to clothing, you reduce the demand for fast fashion and its environmental impact.

7.6 Minimalist Living: A Green Approach to Home Design

Explore minimalist living as a green approach to home design. Declutter your living spaces to embrace simplicity and functionality. Minimalist design not only creates a serene home environment but also reduces the need for excess resources and furnishings.

7.7 Sustainable Donation and Resale: Extending Product Lifecycles

Opt for sustainable donation and resale options when parting with items. Ensure that your unwanted belongings find new homes, extending their lifecycle and reducing the demand for new products. Contribute to a circular economy that minimizes waste.

7.8 Composting Organic Clutter: From Kitchen to Garden

Integrate composting into your decluttering routine, especially in the kitchen. Turn organic waste into nutrient-rich compost that can be used to enhance your garden or potted plants. This sustainable practice reduces the environmental impact of food waste.

7.9 Energy-Efficient Decluttering: Unplug and Conserve

Practice energy-efficient decluttering by unplugging and conserving energy. Consider the environmental impact of electronic clutter and make a conscious effort to power down devices when not in use. This simple action contributes to energy conservation and sustainability.

7.10 Mindful Consumer Choices: Decluttering Beyond Your Home

Conclude the chapter by adopting mindful consumer choices that extend beyond your immediate surroundings. Be conscious of the environmental impact of your purchases, opting for sustainable and ethically produced items. Consider the lifecycle of products as you declutter your space and make future purchasing decisions.

As you immerse yourself in the detailed strategies of Chapter 7, envision the transformation of your decluttered space into a beacon of sustainability. By embracing eco-friendly practices and making mindful choices, your decluttering journey becomes a positive force for both your home and the planet.

Here are 20 bonus tips to complement the strategies outlined in Chapter 7 and enhance your sustainable decluttering journey:

Eco-Friendly Cleaning Products:

Transition to eco-friendly cleaning products to maintain a green and sustainable cleaning routine as you declutter.

Digital Decluttering:

Extend your decluttering efforts to digital spaces by organizing files, deleting unnecessary emails, and optimizing your digital footprint.

Community Swaps and Share Events:

Participate in community swaps or share events to exchange items with neighbors, reducing the need for new purchases.

Eco-Conscious Packaging:

Choose products with minimal and eco-conscious packaging to reduce waste and environmental impact.

Sustainable Art and Decor:

Opt for sustainably sourced or locally crafted art and decor to add personality to your space without contributing to mass production.

Reusable Storage Containers:

Utilize reusable storage containers made from materials like glass or stainless steel to minimize reliance on single-use plastics.

Green Energy Sources:

Consider switching to green energy sources for your home to reduce your carbon footprint during and after the decluttering process.

Upcycled Furniture DIY:

Engage in DIY projects to upcycle furniture, giving old pieces a new life and preventing them from ending up in landfills.

Sustainable Shelving:

Choose sustainable materials for shelving, such as reclaimed wood or bamboo, to enhance your storage solutions.

Energy-Efficient Lighting:

Upgrade to energy-efficient LED lighting to save energy and contribute to a sustainable home environment.

Buy Secondhand:

Explore secondhand stores or online marketplaces for items you need instead of buying new, reducing demand for new production.

Green Textiles:

Choose eco-friendly textiles for bedding and linens, such as organic cotton or bamboo, to support sustainable and ethical practices.

Local Farmers' Market:

Purchase fresh produce from local farmers' markets to support local agriculture and reduce the environmental impact of long-distance transportation.

Zero-Waste Grocery Shopping:

Embrace zero-waste grocery shopping by using reusable bags, containers, and buying items in bulk to minimize packaging waste.

Mindful Water Consumption:

Be mindful of water consumption during your decluttering process. Collect rainwater for plants and consider water-saving devices.

DIY Natural Cleaners:

Create your own natural cleaning solutions using ingredients like vinegar and baking soda to reduce reliance on chemical cleaners.

Green Transportation:

Consider sustainable transportation options, such as biking or walking, when disposing of items or running errands related to decluttering.

Regenerative Gardening:

If you have outdoor space, practice regenerative gardening techniques to enhance soil health and promote biodiversity.

Sustainable Art Storage:

If storing artwork, use acid-free and archival materials to ensure the long-term preservation of valuable pieces.

E-Waste Recycling:

Responsibly dispose of electronic waste by recycling old gadgets and devices through certified e-waste recycling programs.

Incorporating these bonus tips into your sustainable decluttering efforts will not only benefit your immediate surroundings but also contribute to a more environmentally conscious and eco-friendly lifestyle.

Chapter 8- Maintaining Your Decluttered Home

In Chapter 8, our focus shifts to the crucial aspect of maintaining the serenity and order you've cultivated through the decluttering journey. Explore practical and sustainable strategies that ensure your home remains a harmonious haven over time. From daily habits to seasonal routines, this chapter guides you in sustaining the decluttered lifestyle you've worked hard to achieve.

8.1 Daily Decluttering Rituals: Micro-Moments of Order

Embark on a journey of daily decluttering rituals—small, intentional actions that prevent clutter from accumulating. Discover micro-moments of order, such as tidying up surfaces, putting items back in their designated places, and maintaining the simplicity you've cultivated.

8.2 Mindful Consumption: Curating Future Belongings

Cultivate a mindset of mindful consumption to prevent future clutter. Approach new purchases with discernment, considering whether an item aligns with your values, serves a purpose, and integrates seamlessly into your decluttered space.

8.3 Seasonal Refresh: A Time for Reevaluation

Incorporate seasonal refreshes into your maintenance routine. Use these moments to reassess your belongings, make adjustments to your organization systems, and address any new items that have entered your home. Embrace the cyclical nature of decluttering to keep your space dynamic and responsive to your evolving needs.

8.4 Decluttering as a Family Ritual: Involving Everyone

Transform decluttering into a family ritual by involving all household members. Foster a sense of shared responsibility, teach decluttering skills to children, and create a collaborative environment where everyone contributes to maintaining a clutter-free home.

8.5 Sustainable Cleaning Practices: Green Maintenance

Integrate sustainable cleaning practices into your maintenance routine. Explore eco-friendly cleaning products, DIY cleaning solutions, and consider reusable cleaning tools to minimize the environmental impact of your cleaning rituals.

8.6 Digital Detox Days: Unplugging for Balance

Incorporate digital detox days into your maintenance plan. Designate specific days where you intentionally unplug from electronic devices, fostering a balanced and mindful relationship with technology within your decluttered home.

8.7 Regular Donation Drives: Continuous Giving

Organize regular donation drives within your community. Use these events to declutter items that are still in good condition but no longer serve you. Create a cycle of continuous giving and keep the flow of your decluttering efforts outward.

8.8 Storage Reevaluation: Adapting to Changing Needs

Periodically reevaluate your storage solutions to adapt to changing needs. Whether due to lifestyle changes or evolving preferences, flexible storage allows your home to remain accommodating and decluttered.

8.9 Decluttering Accountability Partners: Mutual Support

Engage in decluttering accountability partnerships. Connect with friends or family members who share similar decluttering goals. Regular check-ins and mutual support can reinforce your commitment to maintaining a clutter-free environment.

8.10 Mindful Decor Additions: Thoughtful Enhancements

When adding new decor elements, adopt a mindful approach. Choose pieces that align with your decluttered aesthetic, contribute positively to your living space, and enhance the serenity you've established.

8.11 Seasonal Wardrobe Rotations: Clothing Consciousness

Implement seasonal wardrobe rotations to ensure your closet remains streamlined. As the seasons change, assess your clothing and accessories, making intentional choices about what to keep, donate, or store.

8.12 Sustainability Audits: Monitoring Green Practices

Conduct sustainability audits as part of your home maintenance routine. Assess the eco-friendliness of your habits, products, and practices, making adjustments to align with a more sustainable and environmentally conscious lifestyle.

8.13 Decluttering Reflection Journal: Tracking Progress

Maintain a decluttering reflection journal to track your progress and experiences. Use this journal to celebrate achievements, jot down insights, and document any challenges faced during the maintenance phase.

8.14 Mindful Events Planning: Intentional Gatherings

When planning events or gatherings, approach them with mindfulness. Consider the impact on your living space, opt for sustainable hosting practices, and ensure that the essence of your decluttered home is preserved.

8.15 Personal Decluttering Challenges: Continuous Growth

Engage in personal decluttering challenges to foster continuous growth. Set periodic goals, such as decluttering a specific area or reducing possessions by a certain percentage, to maintain momentum and prevent complacency.

8.16 DIY Repairs and Upkeep: Cherishing Possessions

Learn basic DIY repairs and upkeep to extend the life of your possessions. Whether it's fixing a loose screw or repainting furniture, taking care of your belongings adds value and reduces the need for replacements.

8.17 Mindful Purchasing Intentions: Conscientious Shopping

Approach future purchases with conscientious intentions. Prioritize quality over quantity, invest in durable items, and align each purchase with the principles of mindful consumption and a decluttered lifestyle.

8.18 Green Landscaping: Sustainable Outdoor Spaces

Extend your decluttering efforts to outdoor spaces through green landscaping. Create sustainable gardens, use eco-friendly materials for outdoor furniture, and foster an environment that complements the clutter-free ethos of your home.

8.19 Decluttering Celebrations: Milestone Acknowledgment

Celebrate decluttering milestones with intention. Acknowledge the progress you've made, express gratitude for your decluttered home, and use these celebrations as moments of reflection and motivation.

8.20 Community Sustainability Initiatives: Active Participation

Engage in community sustainability initiatives as part of your commitment to maintaining a decluttered and environmentally conscious lifestyle. Participate in local clean-up events, conservation projects, or other initiatives that contribute to a sustainable future for your community.

As you embrace the practices outlined in Chapter 8, envision a home that not only remains decluttered but also becomes a living testament to sustainable living—a space where mindfulness, purposeful choices, and continual growth coalesce to nurture both your immediate environment and the planet.

Here are 20 bonus tips to enhance your efforts in maintaining a decluttered and sustainable home:

Green Energy Audit:

Conduct a green energy audit to identify opportunities for energy efficiency in your home, such as switching to LED bulbs or improving insulation.

Ethical Clothing Swaps:

Participate in ethical clothing swaps within your community to refresh your wardrobe sustainably.

Mindful Water Conservation:

Practice mindful water conservation by fixing leaks, collecting rainwater for plants, and using water-saving appliances.

DIY Natural Home Cleaners:

Create DIY natural cleaners using ingredients like vinegar, baking soda, and essential oils for a chemical-free and eco-friendly cleaning routine.

Energy-Efficient Appliances:

Invest in energy-efficient appliances to reduce your carbon footprint and lower utility bills.

Eco-Friendly Planters:

Use eco-friendly planters made from recycled materials or natural fibers for your indoor plants.

Zero-Waste Grocery Shopping Bags:

Opt for reusable and eco-friendly grocery shopping bags to reduce single-use plastic waste.

Sustainable Paperless Practices:

Transition to paperless billing, note-taking, and documentation to minimize paper consumption.

Eco-Conscious Commuting:

Explore eco-conscious commuting options, such as carpooling, biking, or using public transportation.

Sustainable Gift Wrapping:

Embrace sustainable gift wrapping by using reusable fabric, newspaper, or recycled paper.

Mindful Eating Habits:

Practice mindful eating habits, reduce food waste, and consider composting organic kitchen waste.

Natural Air Purifiers:

Introduce natural air purifiers like indoor plants to enhance air quality in your home.

Sustainable Furniture Pads:

Use furniture pads made from sustainable materials to protect floors and surfaces.

Reusable Coffee Cups and Water Bottles:

Carry reusable coffee cups and water bottles to reduce single-use plastic waste while on the go.

DIY Composting Bin:

Set up a DIY composting bin for organic kitchen waste to create nutrient-rich soil for your plants.

Seasonal Local Produce:

Prioritize seasonal and local produce to support sustainable agriculture and reduce the carbon footprint of your meals.

Eco-Friendly Pet Care:

Choose eco-friendly pet care products and sustainable pet accessories for your furry companions.

Repair Workshops:

Attend repair workshops or learn basic repair skills to extend the life of household items and reduce unnecessary replacements.

Energy-Efficient Window Treatments:

Install energy-efficient window treatments to regulate temperature and reduce the need for excessive heating or cooling.

Community Environmental Initiatives:

Get involved in community environmental initiatives such as tree planting, neighborhood clean-ups, or local conservation projects.

Incorporating these bonus tips into your daily routine will further enrich your commitment to maintaining a decluttered, sustainable, and eco-friendly home.

Conclusion

As we conclude this transformative journey through the art of decluttering and embracing sustainability, take a moment to reflect on the profound changes you've made within the spaces you call home. The commitment to decluttering goes beyond the mere act of organizing belongings; it is a testament to your dedication to cultivating a life of simplicity, intentionality, and sustainability.

Through the eight chapters, you've explored the intricacies of decluttering every facet of your living environment—from physical spaces to digital landscapes, from mindful consumption to sustainable practices. The journey has been more than just a reorganization; it's been a conscious choice to reshape your surroundings and, by extension, your life.

In the pursuit of decluttering, you've not only liberated your physical spaces but also your mind, allowing tranquility to permeate every corner of your existence. The mindful approach to consumption has shifted the narrative from excess to essence, emphasizing the value of intentional living and cherishing what truly matters.

Sustainability has been woven into the fabric of your decluttered lifestyle, creating a harmonious connection between your personal sanctuary and the planet. By adopting eco-friendly practices, making mindful choices, and engaging in sustainable habits, you've become a steward of a greener and more sustainable future.

As you move forward, remember that maintaining a decluttered and sustainable home is a continuous journey—a cycle of growth, reflection, and refinement. Regularly revisit the principles outlined in these chapters, adapt them to your evolving needs, and embrace the dynamic nature of intentional living.

Celebrate the milestones you've achieved, both big and small. Whether it's a clutter-free room, a sustainable habit adopted, or a mindful purchasing decision, each step contributes to the overall tapestry of your transformed lifestyle.

This isn't just the end of a guide; it's the beginning of a new chapter in your life—one marked by the simplicity of spaces, the richness of purpose, and the beauty of sustainability. Carry the lessons learned, the habits formed, and the tranquility gained forward with you, as you continue to shape a home that reflects the essence of who you are and the values you hold dear.

May your decluttered and sustainable lifestyle be a source of inspiration, not only to yourself but to those around you and, collectively, to the world. In this newfound serenity, may you find not only a decluttered home but a sanctuary of peace, purpose, and enduring sustainability.

© **Copyright 2024 by _____Riley Stevens_____ - All rights reserved.**

This document is geared towards providing exact and reliable information in regards to the topic and issue covered. The publication is sold with the idea that the publisher is not required to render accounting, officially permitted, or otherwise, qualified services. If advice is necessary, legal or professional, a practiced individual in the profession should be ordered.

- From a Declaration of Principles which was accepted and approved equally by a Committee of the American Bar Association and a Committee of Publishers and Associations.

In no way is it legal to reproduce, duplicate, or transmit any part of this document in either electronic means or in printed format. Recording of this publication is strictly prohibited and any storage of this document is not allowed unless with written permission from the publisher. All rights reserved.

The information provided herein is stated to be truthful and consistent, in that any liability, in terms of inattention or otherwise, by any usage or abuse of any policies, processes, or directions contained within is the solitary and utter responsibility of the recipient reader. Under no circumstances will any legal responsibility or blame be held against the publisher for any reparation, damages, or monetary loss due to the information herein, either directly or indirectly.

Respective authors own all copyrights not held by the publisher.

The information herein is offered for informational purposes solely, and is universal as so. The presentation of the information is without contract or any type of guarantee assurance.

The trademarks that are used are without any consent, and the publication of the trademark is without permission or backing by the trademark owner. All trademarks and brands within this book are for clarifying purposes only and are the owned by the owners themselves, not affiliated with this document.